Startup Strategy Humor

Startup Strategy Humor

Democratizing Startup Strategy

Rajesh K. Pillania, PhD

BEP BUSINESS EXPERT PRESS

Startup Strategy Humor: Democratizing Startup Strategy

First published in 2018 by
Business Expert Press, LLC
222 East 46th Street, New York, NY 10017
www.businessexpertpress.com

ISBN-13: 978-1-94897-680-0 (paperback)
ISBN-13: 978-1-94897-681-7 (e-book)

Business Expert Press Entrepreneurship and Small Business Management Collection

Collection ISSN: 1946-5653 (print)
Collection ISSN: 1946-5661 (electronic)

Cover and interior design by Exeter Premedia Services Private Ltd., Chennai, India

First edition: 2018

10 9 8 7 6 5 4 3 2 1

Printed in the United States of America.

This book is dedicated to all those who are interested in the challenging but fascinating subject of "startups."

Book with a Social Cause

All royalties earned from this book will be donated to the cause of education.

Disclaimer

This book is a work of fiction and any resemblance with any individual, organization, situation, event, or work is a mere coincidence and the author bears no responsibility for the same.

The author has also used a number of jokes and amusing anecdotes in this book, which he has heard over the years from various people, and he acknowledges all those anonymous contributors.

This book is written in a lighter vein and it doesn't intend to hurt anyone's sentiments or emotions.

Other Books by the Same Author

Strategic Humour: Democratizing Strategy

Love Strategy: A New Perspective on Love, Relationships, Life and Strategy.

Contents

Praise for the Book

A great primer for startups. Thirty concepts have been taken up and explained in the most innovative way. The book covers most of the situations startups likely to face and gives solutions while asking some questions too. A must read for startups and those aspiring to start their own venture.

Mr. Ajai Chowdhry, Founder of HCL, recipient of the
Padma Bhushan award.

Startup Humor is a useful road map for those interested on a startup trek. Through a mix of illustrations, role-plays, and lessons from the real and movie world, this book scopes out some of the challenges and opportunities that entrepreneurs could face when they set up a business for the first time. In an easy and lucid manner, this book inspires, teaches valuable lessons, offers a checklist, and provides important reality checks. A must for those willing to take the plunge.

Mr. Sunil Kant Munjal,
Chairman, Hero Corporate Services & Jt. MD, Hero MotoCorp Ltd.
President, All India Management Association (AIMA) and
Former Chairman, Confederation of Indian Industries (CII).

In its simplicity the book manages to convey pertinent points. No doubt it's being your own boss is a great vision. And bringing it to life, managing, sustaining, scaling requires your 200 percent. Rajesh tries to keep his messaging simple and jargon-free so that we can all relate to the challenges that lie ahead.

Ms. Nita Kapoor,
CEO, India Digital News Ventures of News Corp
(VCCircle Network & Big Decisions).

Startup Humor by Prof. Rajesh K Pillania is an extremely smart book. It's well-structured and is written in a clear, easy-to-read format, with great examples that truly give the reader valuable insights. This book provides very good guidance for people who are just starting their own ventures or those who are in the early stages of their enterprise.

Mr. Praveen Sinha
Angel Investor and Founder of ventures like Jabong,
Aquabrim, Anasha Art

Startup Humor is a wonderful and witty take on the buzzing Indian startup movement. For us to attract and sustain the startup momentum, the paradigm needs to morph to sustainable innovation and IP creation. The book very nicely captures the chaos as well as the opportunity in this ecosystem.

Mr. Sudhir Mehta
Serial Entrepreneur, Chairman Pinnacle Industries.
Co-chair CII National Startup Council

Startup Humor attempts to simplify the multiple challenges that an entrepreneur faces in their own startup journey in a simple, lucid, and entertaining manner. Prof. Rajesh K Pillania's communication style through cartoons is both engaging and thought-provoking to the reader. This style of storytelling helps the reader to connect with the examples quoted against each concept and, in the process, understand them clearly. I would recommend this book to every entrepreneur as it would help them with their anxieties and concerns that they may face and be well prepared for in the future.

Mr. R S Sodhi,
Managing Director, GCMMF Ltd (AMUL)

Startups offer incredible opportunities for people, young and old, to realize their dreams. The startup road is full of potholes that need to be navigated. The journey is tough but the final success of the undertaking is very fulfilling. I hope many startup entrepreneurs will benefit from this book.

Mr. Ashutosh Garg,
Chairman & MD, Guardian Lifecare Pvt. Ltd

Startup Humor succeeds in demystifying the path of a first-time entrepreneurial journey. In an innovative and simple manner the book highlights the pitfalls along the way, how to avoid them and come up with a successful business strategy. A must read for the first-time entrepreneur.

Mr. Jayant Davar
Co-chairman & MD, Sandhar Technologies Limited.

Rajesh's book tackles an important topic, especially for a developing country like India where entrepreneurship is extremely important to continued development. His approach is reader-friendly, engaging, and jargon-free. It will help aspiring entrepreneurs, many of whom might lack formal education, understand key ideas about entrepreneurship. It is a novel and valuable contribution to the literature.

Prof. Nitin Pangarkar,
Academic Director,
MBA Program at National University of Singapore (NUS), NUS,
Singapore.

It is an attempt to extract simple strategy lessons from movies, anecdotes, and common jokes and convey them in a question-answer mode using cartoons between co-founders and strategy professor. The 30 lessons conveyed through simple, non-jargonistic language should be useful tips to first-generation startups. My compliments to him for conveying important lessons in simple style.

Prof. Prem Vrat
Prochancellor and Chief Mentor, The NorthCap University, Gurugram.
Formerly Director, IIT Roorkee; Director-in-charge, IIT Delhi
Professor & Division Chairman, Asian Institute of Technology,
Bangkok.

Preface

Nitish has completed his third year of B.Tech from IIT Delhi, and has gone to stay with his uncle during the summer holidays. His uncle is a Professor of Strategy in a business school. One day, the two started discussing the future career options of Nitish.

Strategy professor: So Nitish, what are your future plans?

Nitish: Regular nine-to-five jobs are not my cup of tea. I want to do something on my own.

Strategy professor: That is good! This is a great time for startups.

Nitish: But I have no idea about startups.

Strategy professor: Yes, that is a common problem. But these days there are so many courses on startups. I can find a good course for you.

Nitish: I don't want to go for an academic course on startups. It could be boring. I want to see some action… some firsthand interaction with the founders of some startups.

Strategy professor: Not an issue. Incidentally, I am going to interact with three founders of a new startup and they happen to be my students. You can attend these meetings as a silent observer when they visit me for discussions.

Nitish: That would be great. Thank you!

Strategy professor: You are welcome.

Acknowledgments

This book wouldn't have been possible without generous inputs from four different startup founders—Aditya, Girdhari, Nimisha, and Asif—and my colleagues at Management Development Institute (MDI), Gurgaon, namely Professors Dhruv and Rohit.

I am grateful to Prof. Nitin Pangarkar, Associate Professor, National University of Singapore Business School, Singapore, and Prof. Sunny Li Sun, PhD, Assistant Professor, The Bloch School of Management, University of Missouri–Kansas City, Kansas City (Missouri), for their valuable inputs.

I am also grateful to Prof. Kiran Momyaya, Professor of Strategy, SJM School of Management, IIT Mumbai, and Prof. Siri Terjesen, Associate Professor, American University, Washington D.C. Metro Area, for encouraging this interesting idea of the book.

I am thankful to Professors Sunil, Madhu Shree, Niva, Anupama, Ankur, Nakul, and Shaphali—my colleagues at Management Development Institute (MDI), Gurgaon—and to FPM Scholar Nupur at MDI, Gurgaon, for reading the first draft and giving their critical and valuable inputs.

Majority of the stories from the book are already shared on Times of India blogs and I am thankful to them. I have also used some jokes in the book, which I have heard over the years from friends, and acknowledge the anonymous creator of those jokes.

Introduction

Globally, "startups" are in vogue these days. In India too, the trend is catching up and the government is also encouraging startups.

Though there is a growing interest in the subject and the number of startups is increasing, there is also a huge mortality rate of startups. Though interest in startups is increasing in India and many people want to go for startups, they stay away from startups for a number of reasons including the complexities involved and the concerns about possible failure.

The purpose of this book is to make it simple and easy to understand startups—with an element of fun thrown in. This book explains 30 concepts related to startups in an innovative way. The author sincerely hopes to bring down the concepts of startups from ivory tower and to demystify and democratize startups for the masses.

The Plot and the Characters

There are three founders of a startup named *uthaepadtae.com*. These three went to the same management school; all of them are in their early 30s.

Before founding their startup they went to their Professor of Strategy in their alma mater and requested him to guide them and lend them a helping hand, and the Professor agreed to help them with his insights and suggestions whenever needed. This book deals with the 30 issues raised by the founders for inputs from the professor.

The reader may read the book from the beginning till the end or choose any topic and read it because each topic is treated as a stand-alone. The discussions among the founders are found on the pages on the left; the inputs from the Professor of Strategy are found on the pages on the right.

CHAPTER 1

Why Startup?

A Car and Dogs

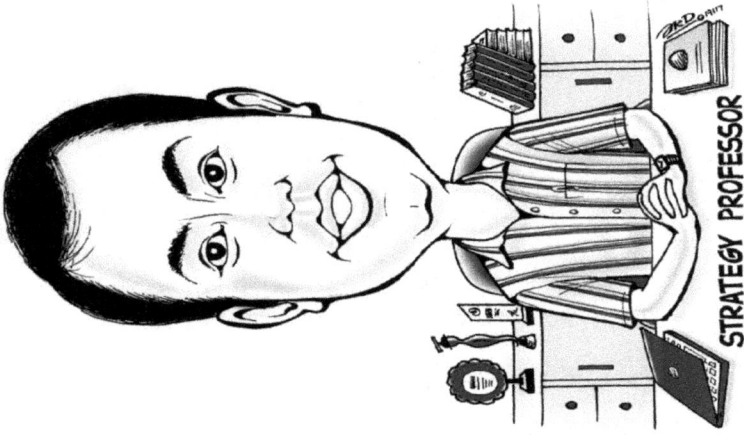

STRATEGY PROFESSOR

You have an interesting situation. Let me share a recent, funny experience I have had.

A few days ago I was going for a morning walk. A car was passing by and a dog started barking and chasing it. Suddenly, from nowhere, many other dogs joined it. After 30 to 40 meters the car stopped and the driver stepped out of the car asking passersby for directions. The dogs too stopped: some stood there for a few seconds, some went away, and some again followed the car for a short distance. I could not understand why they were running after the car in the first place and why they, once they caught up with it, lost their interest it!

Take Away: If you don't know what you want, you would waste time running after anything and everything. Clarity about why you want to go for a startup is very important.

Your Turn Now: What is your reason for startup? Is it at least a bit realistic? How can you improve on it?

CHAPTER 2

What Startup?

From Changing the World to Changing Oneself!

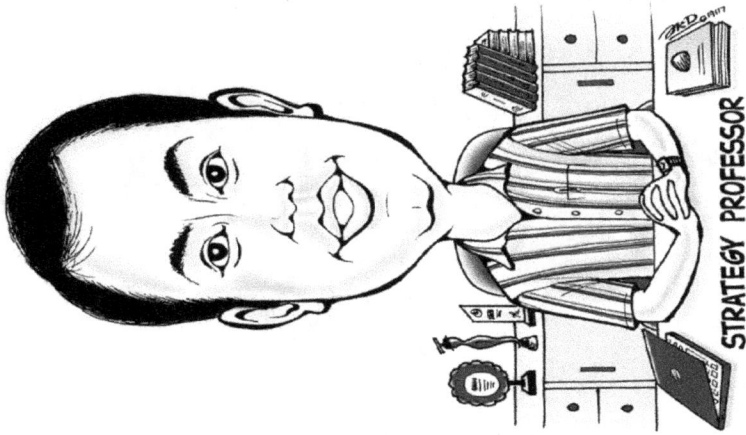

STRATEGY PROFESSOR

Let me share a real-life experience that I went through few years ago.

A middle-aged man left the corporate sector and joined our PhD program. When he joined, he was always talking of solving some big problem through his research. However, soon he realized that while he was spending time reading a lot, his friends were making money and progress in their regular jobs; his wife and children also started complaining. To cut a long story short, he left the PhD program within a few months! Instead of changing the world he changed himself and went back to a regular corporate job!

Take Aways: Startups journey is a tough journey and one has to decide what one wants to do depending on one's resources, capabilities, and limitations. It's good to be ambitious but one has to be at least a bit realistic too.

Your Turn Now: What startup do you want to go for? Is it at least a bit realistic for success? How can you improve on it?

CHAPTER 3

Entrepreneurial Spirit

The Hilarious Case of Ranchodas!

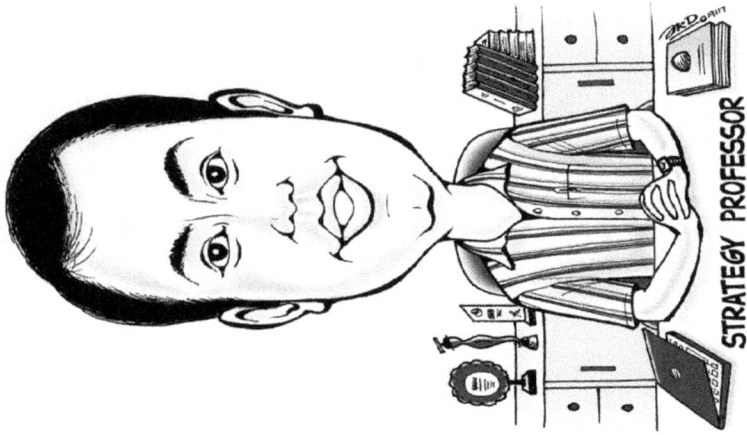

STRATEGY PROFESSOR

You have an interesting question. Let me share an amazing scene from the Hindi movie "3 Idiots."

In the movie, the sister of the heroine was on the verge of delivering a baby but she was unable to reach the hospital due to heavy rains. The hero Aamir Khan and his friends didn't give up; they ensured a smooth delivery despite many challenges: they generated electricity using car batteries during a power cut and made a makeshift vacuum pump from a vacuum cleaner. The hero differed from the ways of the masses and kept challenging the established norms. Not only that, he kept trying to apply the learnings in innovative ways.

Take Aways: A successful entrepreneur has the courage to think differently and has the spirit to fight against all odds to achieve his entrepreneurial dream.

Your Turn Now: Do you think you have an entrepreneurial spirit? Why do you think so? How can you improve on it?

CHAPTER 4

Passion—The Nectar of Startups

The Case of Wrestler Mahavir Singh Phogat!

STARTUP STRATEGY SESSION

I am not sure whether we should take him in our team. How to decide on taking him on board or not?

Yesterday, we met an interesting investor and he wants to join us as a founder.

Well, I don't think it is a great idea.

CO-FOUNDER

CO-FOUNDER

CO-FOUNDER

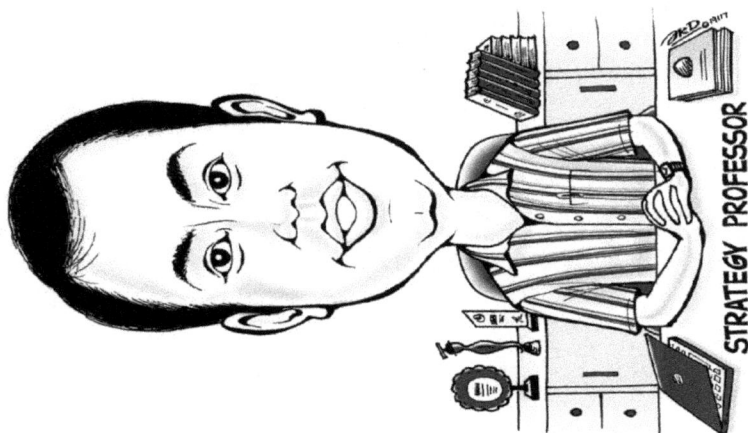

STRATEGY PROFESSOR

It is a critical question. Let me share an interesting lesson from the Hindi movie "Dangal" based on the real-life story of wrestler Mahavir Singh Phogat.

The movie has an important lesson about having passion for one's work. The hero does not have much of resources and social support but is passionate about winning gold medal in international events for India. He fights against all odds to make his daughters international wrestlers and win gold medals for India. One of the important qualities required for a startup is passion in the founders for making the startup a success.

Take Aways: The startup journey is not all hunky dory. It requires passion and commitment to keep moving in the face of adversities and failures.

Your Turn Now: Are you passionate about your startup? Will the passion stay when you encounter hardships? If yes, why do you think so?

CHAPTER 5

Startup Team

Lessons from Aamir Khan in Lagaan

STARTUP STRATEGY SESSION

My wife is curious about the startup and wants to join us. What do you think?

Well, I don't think it is good idea. My wife is already driving me crazy at home!

Maybe they can also join as founders because we trust them. What do you think strategy professor?

CO-FOUNDER

CO-FOUNDER

CO-FOUNDER

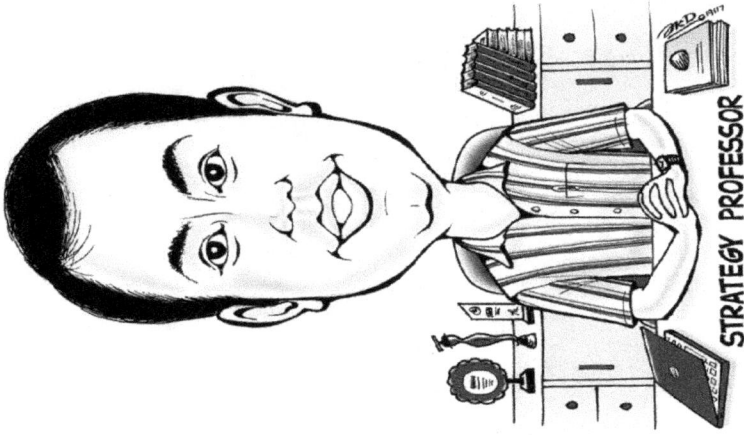

STRATEGY PROFESSOR

You are getting into a trap that many founders often fall into. Having the right team and managing it well is a must for any successful startup. Let me share something interesting from the Hindi movie "Lagaan."

In the movie, the hero Aamir khan assembles a cricket team from people in the village who has never played cricket and has no idea about the game. He manages to win the match against a well-established team! His logic was to choose those people who had the required strengths for the game and many of them had unique and complementary strengths making a great team for the startup in the Cricket game.

Take Aways: Involve only those people who are needed for the success of your startup and have mutually complementary strengths or some unique strength required for success.

Your Turn Now: What is a good team for your startup? Have you chosen your team properly for the success of your startup? Do your team members bring in complementary strengths?

CHAPTER 6

Resilience

Learning from the Hindi Movie Guru!

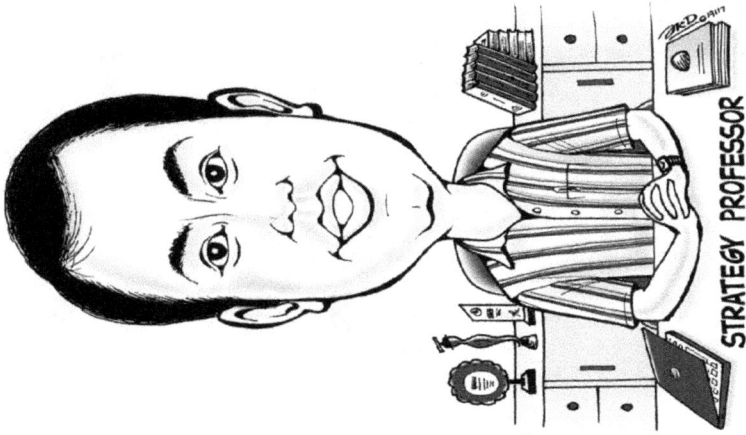

Your team looks good but I have a suggestion for you. Let me share an interesting scene from the Hindi movie "Guru."

There is a courtroom scene and the going seems to be against the protagonist Abhishek Bacchan. He has suffered a paralytic attack and his speech is hampered; but he keeps calm and responds with a lot of conviction during the last part of the trial. In the movie, there are many situations where he remains resilient even in the face of difficulties.

Take Aways: Resilience is one of the main traits of successful startups because the startup journey is full of various kinds of surprises and challenges.

Your Turn Now: Is your team resilient? Why do you think so? How can you improve on it?

CHAPTER 7

Ideation with Innovation

An Incorrigible Drunkard and a Newspaper Advertisement

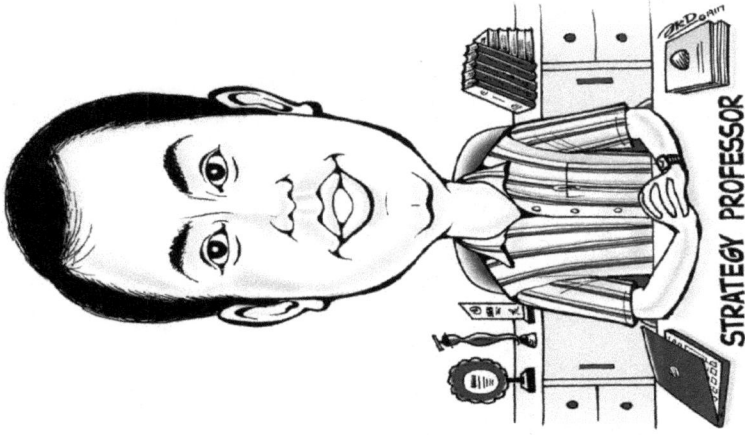

STRATEGY PROFESSOR

All of us are more innovative than we think we are. Let me share a hilarious incident.

There was an advertisement in the newspaper. It said, "Are you an incorrigible drunkard? If yes, call us, we can help you!"

Seeing this advertisement, a wife asked his drunkard husband to call them. The man called them and he couldn't be happier! The advertiser was actually a local liquor shop and was giving information about a discount offer on liquor!

This is hilarious. I am sure now you would agree that we are are more innovative than we think we are.

Take Aways: We are more innovative than we think we are. We should realize that and try to create innovative ideas. However, the ideas have to be tested for defensibility and scalability.

Your Turn now: Are you innovative? What are you doing to be innovative? How can you improve on it?

CHAPTER 8

Medici Effect

Mixing Yoga and Omelet-Making Sessions!

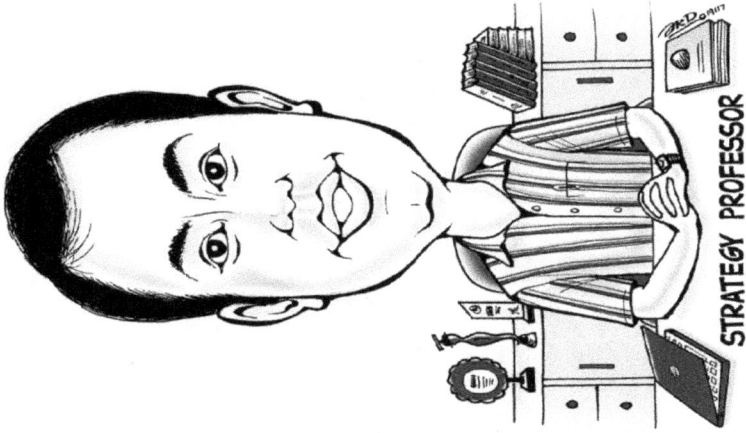

STRATEGY PROFESSOR

There are various approaches for innovation. One popular approach is the Medici Effect. Here is a hilarious incident from the Bollywood movie "Coolie."

The hero (Amitabh Bacchan) had taken the heroine as hostage in a room and he was learning how to cook omelet through a radio program. His back was toward the radio and the heroine, who was tied next to the radio. The heroine played a trick and kept switching the radio between two stations, one for learning yoga and another for learning to cook omelet. This resulted in burning the omelet and entangling the hero in a difficult yoga position. The heroine freed herself from the shackles and left the room using this innovative way.

This is the Medici Effect.

Take Aways: One popular way to innovate is the Medici effect where you bring two different concepts together and at the intersection innovation happens.

Your Turn Now: Are you innovative? Are you using the Medici Effect? How can you use it more?

CHAPTER 9

Opportunity Sensing and Leveraging

Angry White Men and the Rise of Donald Trump!

STARTUP STRATEGY SESSION

I can't agree more. Let's get some ideas on this from our strategy professor.

Our idea has lot of potential and we need to identify the opportunities.

Yes, we have already missed the bus on our last idea by thinking too much. We need to grab the opportunities available before anyone else does.

CO-FOUNDER

CO-FOUNDER

CO-FOUNDER

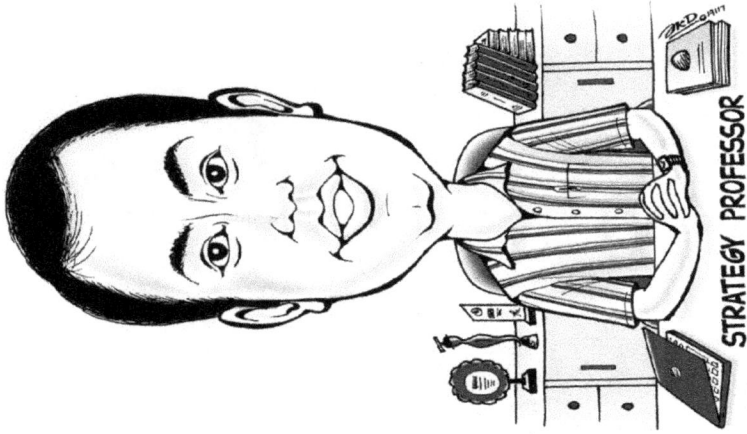

You have an interesting situation. In the recent U.S. elections, Trump was elected President. However, there were not many people who thought that he was going to win the elections.

There were many reasons behind his success. One of the reasons was his understanding of the anger among white men against globalization and the liberal democrats. This was also accepted by the former president Bill Clinton when he said that angry white men were one of the major reasons behind the success of Donald Trump and that Donald Trump knew how to get angry white men to vote for him.

Similarly, an entrepreneur needs to sense an opportunity and leverage it for himself.

Take Aways: Sensing an opportunity and leveraging it to one's own advantage is one of the key skills required for successful startups.

Your Turn Now: How are you going for opportunity sensing and leveraging? Is it correct? How can you improve on it?

CHAPTER 10

Business Model

Learning from a Campus Love Story

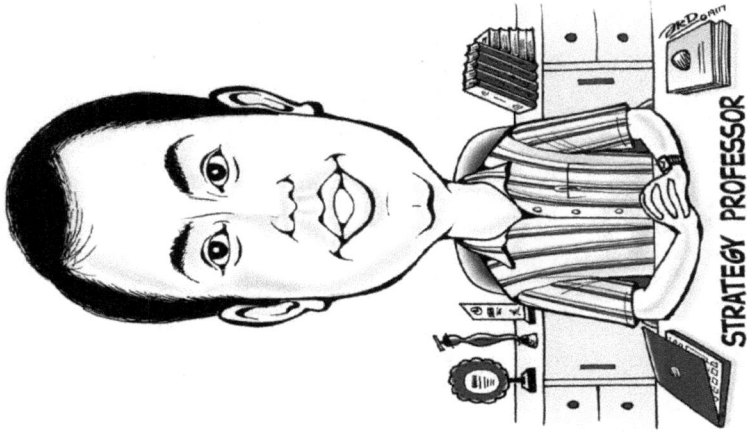

A business model is the way an organization identifies its target customers, creates value for them, and makes some profit out of this. A detailed concept is the business model canvas, which consists of nine blocks.

Let me share an incident from the book "Love Strategy: A New Perspective on Love, Relationships, Life and Strategy."

The "business model" of an MBA student for the love relationship in a management institute is given below.

Key Partners	Key Activities	Value Proposition	Customer Relationship Management	Customer Segment
Friends	Meetings Eating out Movies Keeping himself well groomed and fit; Reinforcing his image and commitment to Charu	Career Security Trust Care Sensitivity Commitment Fun	Compliments Gifts	Charu
	Key Resources Time Efforts Pocket Money		**Delivery** Face to face meetings, Phone calls, Whatsup message, Facebook chat	
Cost Time Efforts Pocket Money			**Revenue** Happiness Satisfaction Relationship	

Take Aways: It is critical to have a correct business model for the success of any startup.

Your Turn now: What is your business model? Is it the right one? What should it be?

CHAPTER 11

Niche Focus & Domain Knowledge for Entry Strategy

Special 26

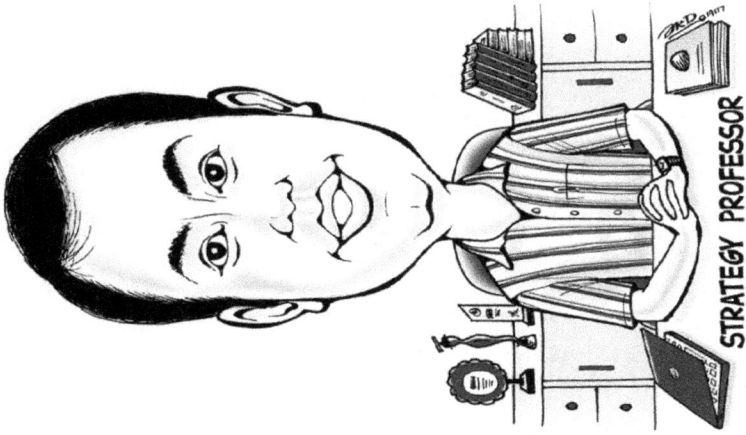

STRATEGY PROFESSOR

You are making the same mistake as many other startups. Let me share an interesting lesson from the Hindi movie "Special 26."

In the movie, a gang of con men loot unethical businessmen and corrupt politicians by posing as Central Bureau of Investigation (CBI) officers.

They have good knowledge of how CBI works and the fear dishonest people have of CBI. So they were quite successful as a startup gang without much competition from others.

Take Aways: It is a good entry strategy to have good knowledge of the trade and to start with a niche segment.

Your Turn Now: Are you targeting a broad market or a niche segment? What is the entry barrier for others? Is it defendable?

CHAPTER 12

Which Product and Market to Go For

Learning from a Campus Love Story

STARTUP STRATEGY SESSION

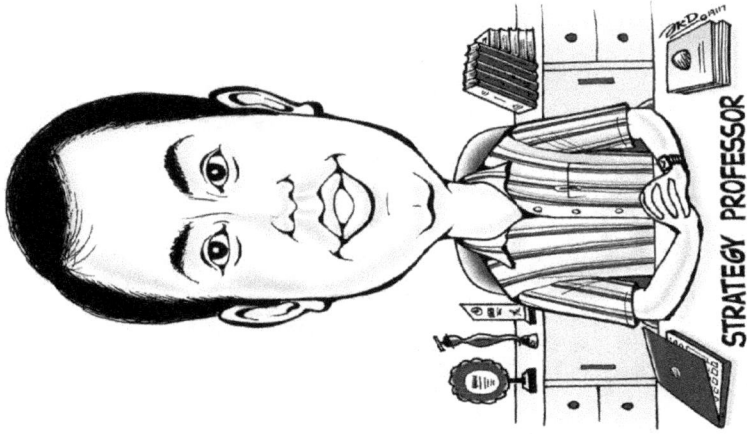

STRATEGY PROFESSOR

Well, it is a very important decision. The Ansoff Matrix gives the various ways in which a company chooses combinations of products and markets. Considering existing markets or new markets on the one hand, and existing products or new products on the other, it creates four possibilities of market penetration, market expansion, product expansion, and diversification.

Let me share a story from the book "Love Strategy: A New Perspective on Love, Relationships, Life and Strategy."

In a management institute, a student Abhishek is looking for a girlfriend but is not successful in finding one in his institute. So he decides to go to a new market (an inter-college cultural festival) with a new product (his newly acquired ability to play the guitar). The Ansoff Matrix for Abhishek is given below.

Markets		New	Inter college cultural festival and without guitar Abhishek	Inter college cultural festival and Abhishek playing guitar
	Existing		CRNP Institute and without guitar Abhishek	CRNP Institute and Abhishek playing guitar
			Existing	New
				Products

Take Aways: It is important to choose the right combination of products and market.

Your Turn Now: What is your Ansoff matrix? Is it the right one for you? What should it be?

CHAPTER 13

Vanity Metrics

Beware of Nondrinker Drivers!

STARTUP STRATEGY SESSION

Our idea is great. Even if we capture 0.5 percent of the big market, we will end up selling to millions.

I also agree. Let's cross-check it with the strategy professor.

Yes, by all conservative estimates, the prospects look good.

CO-FOUNDER

CO-FOUNDER

CO-FOUNDER

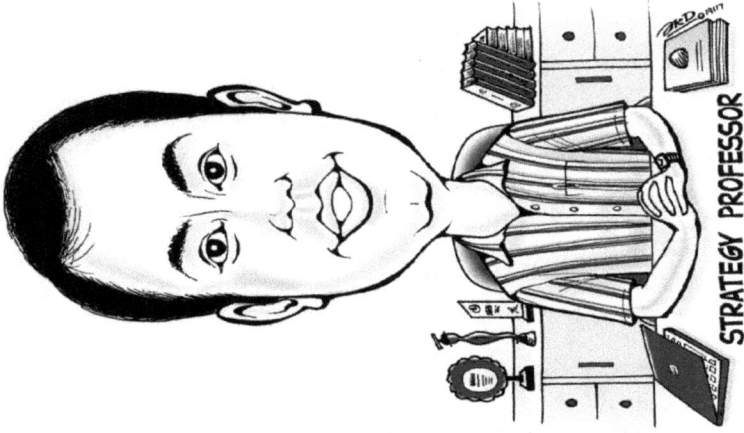

STRATEGY PROFESSOR

Let me share a hilarious situation at a traffic signal.

Fatafat Singh was caught by the Traffic Police for drunken driving.

Traffic Police: You should not drive after drinking. It is so dangerous. A recent study has shown that 23 percent of road accidents are alcohol-related.

Fatafat Singh: Wow! This means that the remaining 77 percent are caused by people who don't drink alcohol! You should catch them because they cause three times more accidents!!!

You may find it hilarious but in reality many aspiring entrepreneurs have this biased view of reality and vanity metrics similar to Mr. Fatafat Singh, and that's why they run into trouble! Vanity metrics are measurements and calculations that look good on paper but are not realistic.

Take Aways: It is important not to go by vanity metrics. An entrepreneur should go by realistic measurable matrices instead.

Your Turn Now: Are you using Vanity Metrics? Why are you doing so? What are the correct metrics you should be using?

CHAPTER 14

Role of Assumptions

Flawed Interpretation of the Environment: "They think I am God!"

STARTUP STRATEGY SESSION

It is a tough challenge to crack. Let's get inputs of strategy professor on this aspect.

The business environment is changing so fast.

Yes, it is beyond our comprehension and predictions.

CO-FOUNDER

CO-FOUNDER

CO-FOUNDER

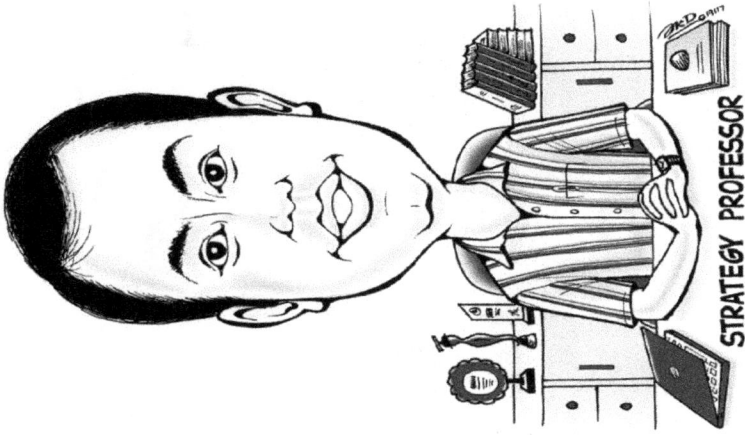

STRATEGY PROFESSOR

Whenever there is a new technology there are too many new entrants and many of these startups fail miserably. It happens because their assumptions of the environment and their own capabilities are flawed.

Let me share a joke.

An irritating and delusional man comes back home after a morning walk in a nearby park. He tells his wife that he is considered to be God by the ladies in the park because whenever he enters the park the ladies say, "God, (he) is here again!"

You might find it weird but ironically many startups have similar assumptions.

Take Aways: Startups should interpret at the environment and their own strengths correctly.

Your Turn Now: What are your assumptions about your environment? Are these assumptions correct? How can you improve on it?

CHAPTER 15

Balance between Analysis and Action

Calculating Laughing Points in a Movie for Marriage!

STARTUP STRATEGY SESSION

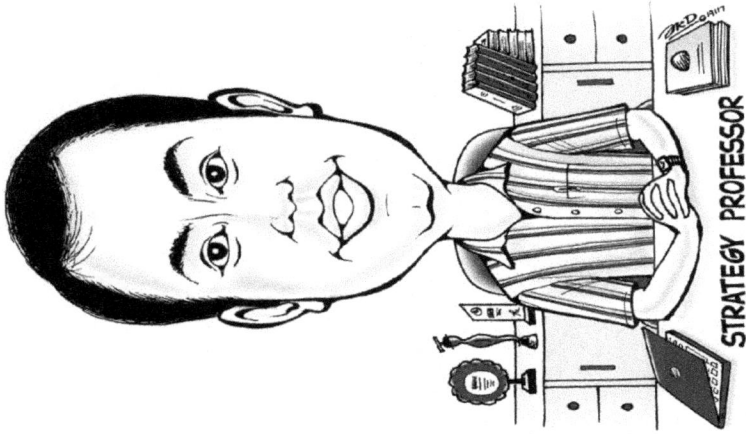

There is a hilarious scene in the movie "Namaste London" where the lead actress Katrina Kaif and her family go to meet a boy in Hyderabad for a marriage proposal.

The boy is busy on his laptop while everyone drinks tea and stares at him. "I am sorry for holding up all of you like this. But I am in the middle of something very important right now," he says.

Rishi Kapoor (Katrina's father) says, "Son, what are you up to? Some important office work, I am sure. It's okay. We understand how demanding work-life can be in India."

Boy: "Not at all. I am just calculating the compatibility index for the girl and me using this brilliant software I have."

Katrina: "WHAT! Really? Don't you think talking to me would help answer this question better?"

Boy: "Oh, yes, of course! I also think we should go watch a movie together."

Rishi Kapoor: (sounding relieved) "Yes, yes, son! Going to the movies is a great way to spend some time together."

Boy: "Well! Uncle, I am talking serious business here. I am going to note down the points in the movie where she laughs and where I laugh. I will get to calculate the index better this way."

Rishi: "Okay! That's it! I think we should leave now. And, by the way, son, if your parents had done all those calculations planning for your birth, you would not be even born today."

Take Aways: It is important to have a bias for action because too much thinking without action leads to paralysis by analysis. A right balance between analysis and action is a must.

Your Turn Now: Do you have the right balance between analysis and action? Why do you think so? What are you doing to achieve this balance?

CHAPTER 16

Strategy

Chak De India

STARTUP STRATEGY SESSION

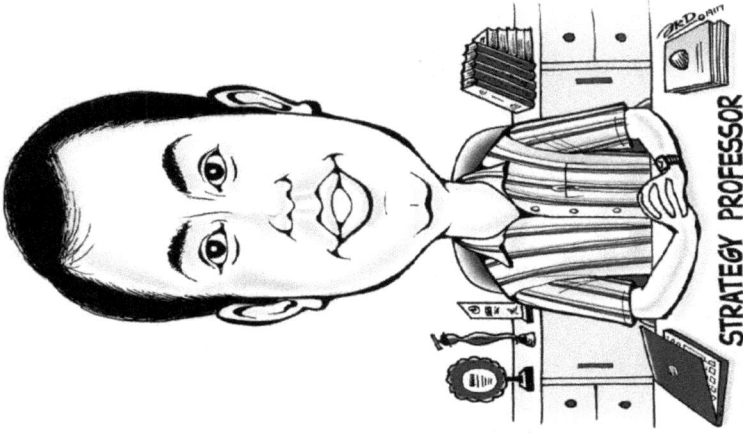

STRATEGY PROFESSOR

Let me share what I have learnt from an interesting Hindi movie "Chak De India."

In the movie, the protagonist Shahrukh Khan is the coach for Indian Women's Hockey team, which was in a pathetic state. It consists of 16 players from different parts of India and he aspires to convert this team into world champions. He uses various strategies to build team spirit and motivate the players: getting resources for the team from the hockey federation, analyzing the strengths and weaknesses of the rival teams, and strategizing for each match. He succeeds in making his team win the world championship.

Take Aways: To be successful, every start up should have a clear strategy and be ready to learn and improve.

Your Turn Now: Do you have a well-defined strategy in place? Does it have the elements of feedback and improvements? How can you improve on it?

CHAPTER 17

Strategic Thinking: The Fine Art of Balancing

Learning Driving without Sitting in the Driver's Seat!

STARTUP STRATEGY SESSION

These days there is a lot of talk about strategic thinking for startups. The challenges that startups face require a lot of strategic thinking.

Developing strategic thinking is a big challenge. Most of us are so much into firefighting and operations management, that we find no time for strategic thinking. We often do not realize that strategic thinking eliminates the need for most firefighting! Let's see what our strategy professor has to say about strategic thinking.

I think it is all jargon and waste of time. We should focus on the product and technology.

CO-FOUNDER

CO-FOUNDER

CO-FOUNDER

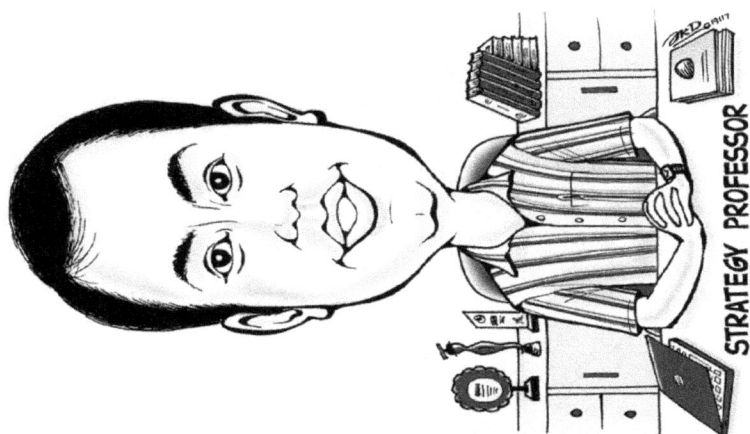

STRATEGY PROFESSOR

Let me share an interesting story.

Ten days ago I bought a new car. I hired a driving school to teach me how to drive a car. On the first day came a guy from the driving school claiming to be an expert in electrical components and explained about the various electrical components in the car. On the second day came a guy claiming to be an expert in mechanical systems and told me about the various mechanical systems in the car. On the third day came a guy claiming to be an expert in car interiors and told me about the interiors of the car and went back.

It continued for a week, without any discussion or practice of actual car driving!

Most of us will find it crazy and some might find it hilarious too!

But, wait a second: are not many of the people working in startups behaving in the same way?

Take Aways: It is certainly important to have some idea about the various components of a car but one should more importantly know how to drive it.

Similarly in any organization, every activity and every department has a role to play but the organization as a whole has to achieve what it aspires for, that is, it has to follow its strategy; all the activities and departments must look at the bigger picture too. So it is important to look at both the big picture and the small picture and find the right balance.

Your Turn Now: Do you have strategic thinking? What are you doing to develop strategic thinking? How can you improve it?

CHAPTER 18

Organizational Culture

Culture Eats Strategy for Breakfast—Drucker

STARTUP STRATEGY SESSION

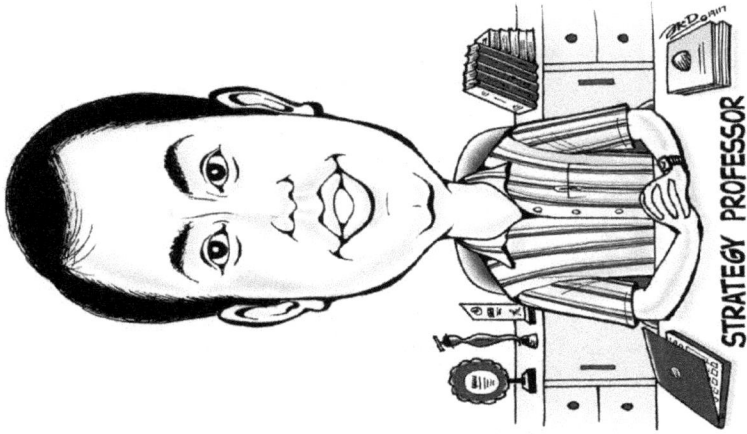

STRATEGY PROFESSOR

Let me share an interesting incident.

It is common knowledge that many people in the public sector banks in India were not very work-oriented and efficient. These banks offered a voluntary retirement scheme to improve performance by weeding out the inefficient, and, to the surprise and utter dismay of the banks, many of the competent people took up the offer and joined private banks!

Take Aways: Organizational culture matters the most for creating a successful startup. It has to focus on elements of ownership and fairness and also focus on continuous learning and growth opportunities for its employees.

Your Turn Now: Are you able to attract great talent for your startup? What is your strategy for organizational culture? How are you ensuring learning and growth opportunities?

CHAPTER 19

Marketing Strategy

Success of "Brand Modi" in Parliament Elections 2014

STARTUP STRATEGY SESSION

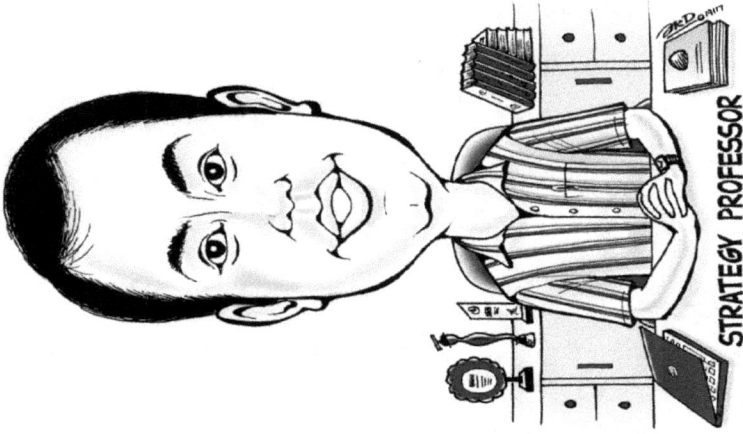

STRATEGY PROFESSOR

Well, you are falling into the same trap as the one many startup founders are falling into.

In the recent past, one major marketing strategy success is that of Brand Modi in 2014 general elections. The team of Modi did a number of right things while building brand Modi using his Gujarat story; using catchy slogans, implementing a master communication strategy to reach out to the masses, and so on. The key differentiator in the elections was Brand Modi built over a good marketing strategy. The victory of Narendra Modi and BJP in the 2014 general elections is a classic case for learning marketing strategy!

Take Aways: Technology is important but it is important to have a good marketing strategy in place.

Your Turn Now: What is your marketing strategy? Is it good enough? How can you improve on it?

CHAPTER 20

Social Media per se Is Not Marketing Strategy

Please Update My Facebook Status as "DEAD!"

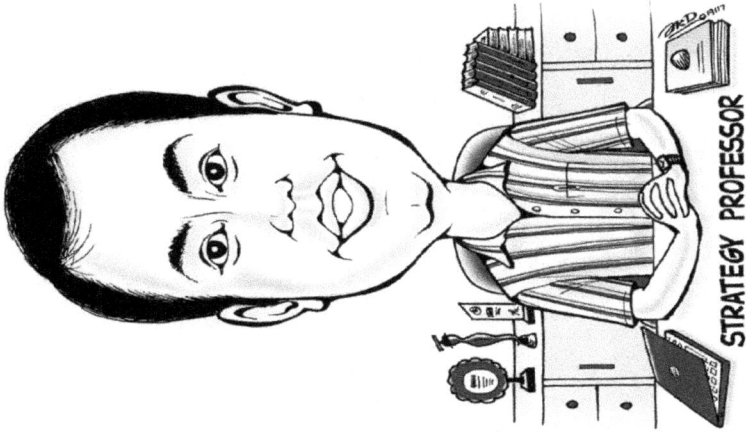

STRATEGY PROFESSOR

Hold on for a second. Sometimes we get addicted to certain things so much that we miss the big picture. This crazy incident from the book "Strategic Humour: Democratising Strategy" will make it clear.

Padtae Uthtae killed the bar owner and he was sentenced to life. Before being hanged, the prison warden asks if he has a last wish. Padtae Uthtae replies, "Please update my Facebook status as 'DEAD'."

This is really crazy!

Take Aways: Social media, though very powerful, is just one more medium of communication and exploring it should be in sync with—and not independent of—the overall marketing strategy.

Your Turn Now: Do you have a social media strategy? Is it in sync with your marketing and overall strategy? How can you improve on it?

CHAPTER 21

Pitch!

Rang De Basanti Screen Test

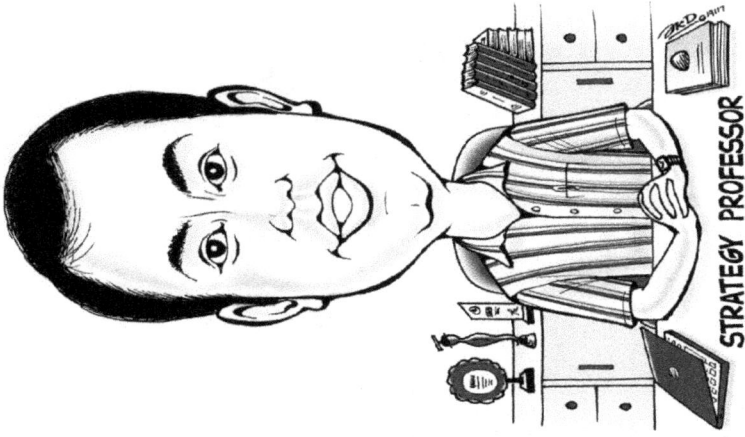

STRATEGY PROFESSOR

You have an interesting discussion. Let me share a hilarious incident.

In the famous Hindi movie "Rang De Basanti" there is a scene in which the director is looking for actors for a movie on Indian freedom fighters. A number of people appear for the screen test and the scene is hilarious because even the basics of acting are missing among the aspirants! The situation from the perspective of an investor is similar since many crucial things are missing or are not conveyed properly in the pitch by startups!

Take Aways: Your pitch must be comprehensive, short, and interesting from the perspective of a potential investor.

Your Turn Now: Is your pitch comprehensive, short, and interesting from the perspective of a prospective investor? Why do you think so? How can you improve on it?

CHAPTER 22

Financial Strategy

Two and a Half Men

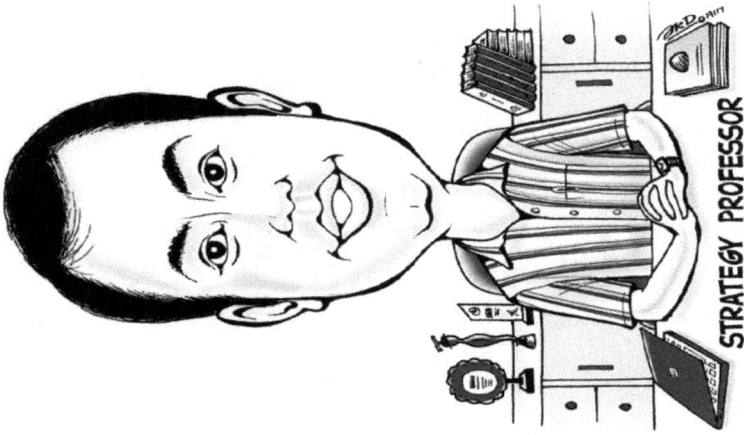

STRATEGY PROFESSOR

Here is an incident you can benefit from.

In one of the episodes of Two and a Half Men, one of the main characters—Alan—collects money from his relatives and friends in the name of a bogus investment scheme to fulfill his desire for luxury. Some startup founders too do the same thing. But investors are more wary these days.

Take Aways: There is more money in the market than are good ideas for startups. The focus of financial strategy should be on adding and delivering value. Now investors demand that one should deliver results first—before investing in unnecessary luxuries like an expensive car, an impressive office, and so on!

Your Turn Now: Do you have a financial strategy? Are you focusing on delivering results or on investing in unproductive luxuries? What should be your financial strategy for adding and delivering value?

CHAPTER 23

Crowd Sourcing

The Rise of AAP and Arvind Kejriwal

STARTUP STRATEGY SESSION

I have heard about crowd sourcing. Let's get some inputs on this from strategy professor.

It is getting difficult to raise funds from investors.

I don't get this. After all, we have such a great business idea! What are other funding options we have?

CO-FOUNDER

CO-FOUNDER

CO-FOUNDER

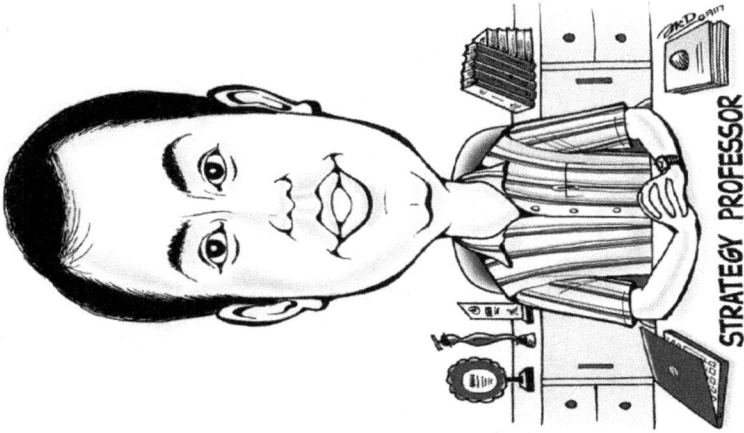

STRATEGY PROFESSOR

Let me share with you a recent interesting development in India.

In India, entering into politics requires a lot of money. Established political parties can generate the huge resources required for politics. Aam Admi Party (AAP) was an exception and, in the initial days, AAP got its money from ordinary people—and the individual contributions were often very small. This is one example of crowd sourcing.

Take Aways: There are platforms available for crowd sourcing for almost everything including startups. Besides crowd sourcing, there are other popular options such as bootstrapping, angel investors, and venture capital; your choice shall be determined by your overall strategy and your financial strategy.

Your Turn Now: Are you planning to go for crowd sourcing? Why should people give you money through crowd sourcing? How can you improve on it?

CHAPTER 24

Staying Focused

The Interesting Case of AAP!

STARTUP STRATEGY SESSION

Yes that sounds exciting! We shall seek the advice of our strategy professor about our plans for market expansion.

We have made an entry into Delhi. There are similar opportunities in other metro cities and we should move fast.

Why metro cities only? Even two-tier and three-tier cities present good opportunities for growth and we should try to capture as much market as possible.

CO-FOUNDER

CO-FOUNDER

CO-FOUNDER

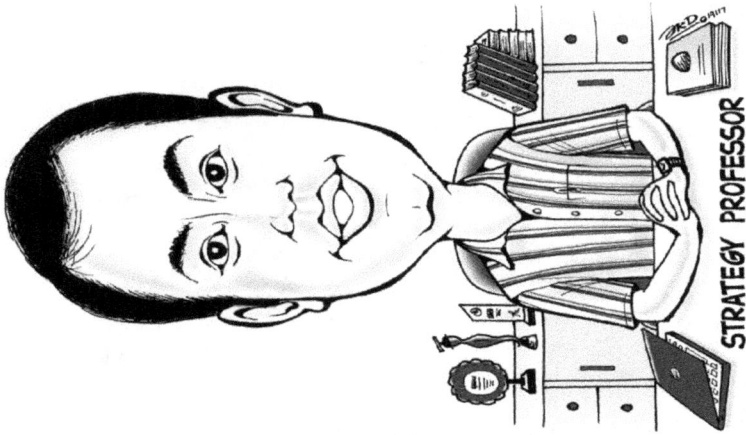

This is a very critical situation that many startups face and often end up on the wrong side. Let me share an interesting example.

Aam Aadmi Party (AAP) got phenomenal success in Delhi assembly elections in 2014. Instead of first delivering on the high expectations and staying focused on Delhi, they went for national elections, and then the state elections in Punjab and Goa. They lost in all these elections. Not only that, eventually they ended up losing a by-election in Delhi and the Delhi Municipal Elections too!

This is a classic case of growth trap that many startups fall into.

Take Aways: It is very important to stay focused and stay away from growth trap.

Your Turn Now: Are you focused? What are you doing to ensure staying away from growth trap? What are you doing to ensure this in future also?

CHAPTER 25

Implementation Challenges

The Days after the Honeymoon

What do you mean? I have left my job trusting you and now you are showing your true colors!

I have contributed so much for this startup but now it all looks like wasted effort. You people are not contributing as much as I am.

Can you please stop fighting! We are running into challenges and your continuous fighting and blame games are making things difficult. Let's get some solution from our strategy professor.

STARTUP STRATEGY SESSION

CO-FOUNDER

CO-FOUNDER

CO-FOUNDER

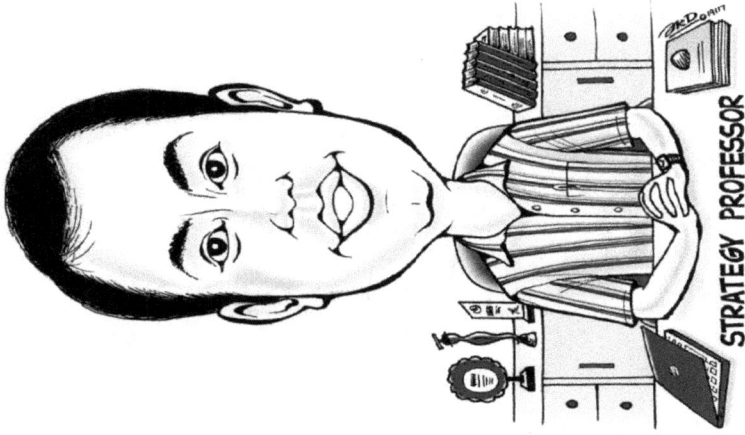

STRATEGY PROFESSOR

It's not good to see you bickering and fighting. But don't be upset, it happens in many startups.

Let me share an interesting perspective.

Everything looks great before going for a love marriage as both the partners are brought together by the dreams of living together with someone they love! However, many of these marriages face rough waters after the honeymoon—and, sometimes, during the honeymoon too!

A man who was fighting a divorce case after a love marriage goes to a saint asking for feedback; and the saint quipped that he should ask his wife instead because she could list an infinite number of faults dating back to his previous births too!

Take Aways: It is important to visualize a startup journey in its totality before jumping into it. There are numerous problems of implementation as well as unseen challenges, which are inevitable; one should be ready to face such challenges.

Your Turn Now: Are you prepared for possible problems of implementation as well as unseen challenges in the startup journey? Have you put some mechanism or understanding in place to tackle these challenges? How can you improve on it?

CHAPTER 26

Pivot

The Curious Case of Tendulkar and Kumble

STARTUP STRATEGY SESSION

The angel investor is suggesting pivoting our almost failed startup.

But this kills the basic idea of our startup.

You have a point but that's our only chance of staying in this startup business. Let's see what strategy professor has to say about this.

CO-FOUNDER

CO-FOUNDER

CO-FOUNDER

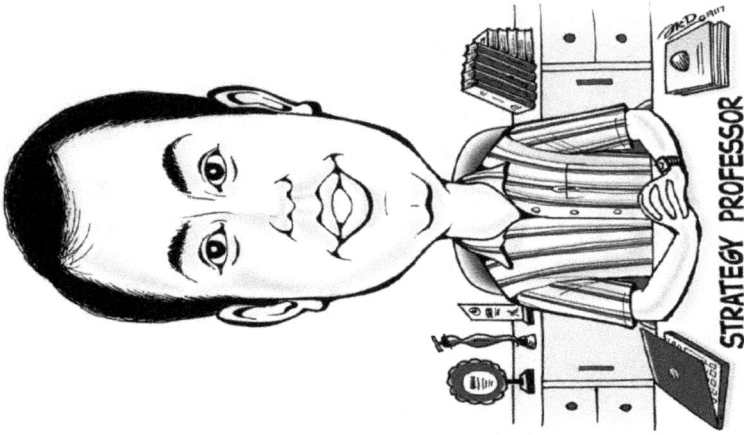

STRATEGY PROFESSOR

You are in a difficult situation. Let me share two interesting examples.

Sachin Tendulkar wanted to be a fast bowler and Anil Kumble wanted to be a batsman. But both listened to the right advice and continued their passion for cricket as a batsman and bowler, respectively!

Take Aways: One needs to be passionate about the idea but needs to be open to feedback and even to pivot when it is not working after reasonable effort.

Your Turn Now: Are you madly, blindly besotted with your startup idea? Is it coming in the way of the success of your startup? Are you mentally prepared for a possible pivot in your startup?

CHAPTER 27

Beware of Startup Myths

Running away with the Passbook Vending Machine instead of the ATM!

STARTUP STRATEGY SESSION

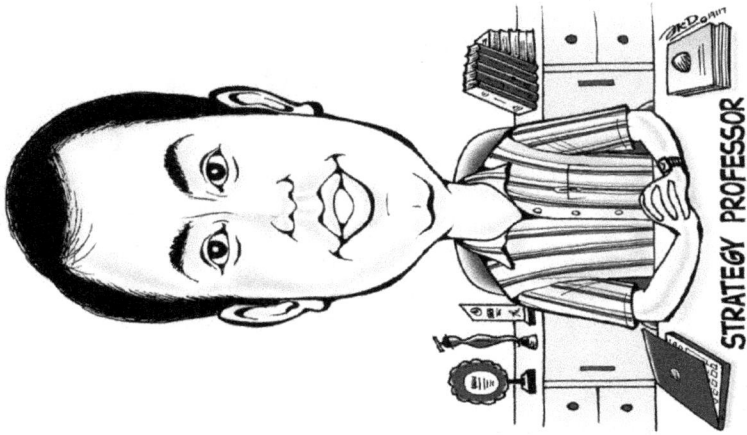

STRATEGY PROFESSOR

There are many myths around startups, and that creates a lot of trouble. Here is a recent story that I shared with Business Insider.

In recent news, some thieves ran away with a passbook vending machine instead of an ATM and, adding insult to injury, were caught in the process!

You will laugh at their silly ignorance but in reality many startups do make such silly mistakes assuming that entrepreneurship is synonymous with reckless risk! Contrary to popular perception, as explained by the great management guru Peter F. Drucker, an entrepreneur is not someone who takes risk.

Take Aways: An entrepreneur minimizes his risk by getting the basics right and remains open-minded to identify/accept his/her mistakes, and keeps learning and improving.

Your Turn Now: Are you following startup sayings blindly? Do you have any mechanism to cross-check these sayings? How can you improve on it?

CHAPTER 28

Hedging the Risk

Take a Bus Home after Getting Drunk!

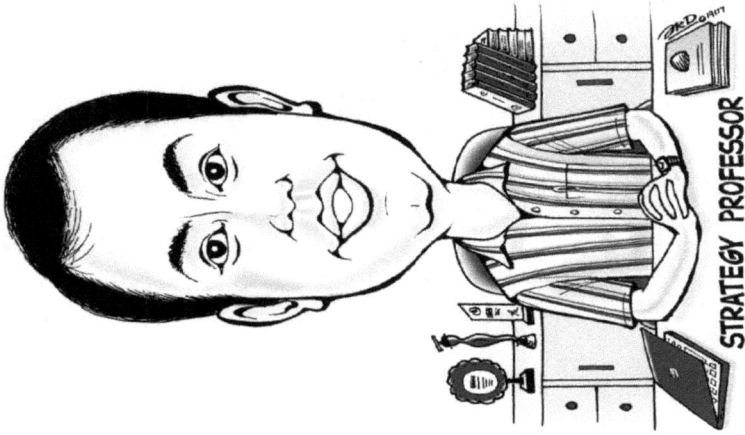

Let me share a funny incident with you.

A guy is advised not to mix drinking and driving.

Next day, after getting drunk, he leaves his car in the parking of the pub and takes a bus home.

In the morning he realizes that he had actually driven a bus home!!!

Ha ha. It is hilarious. On a serious note, many aspiring entrepreneurs adopt the same approach for hedging risk and end up creating complicated situations for themselves.

Take Aways: It is important to hedge the risk but it should not end up increasing your problems!

Your Turn Now: Are you using Hedging for risk? How are you doing it? What is the correct hedging you should be using?

CHAPTER 29

Social Entrepreneurship

The Case of Anna Hazare

STARTUP STRATEGY SESSION

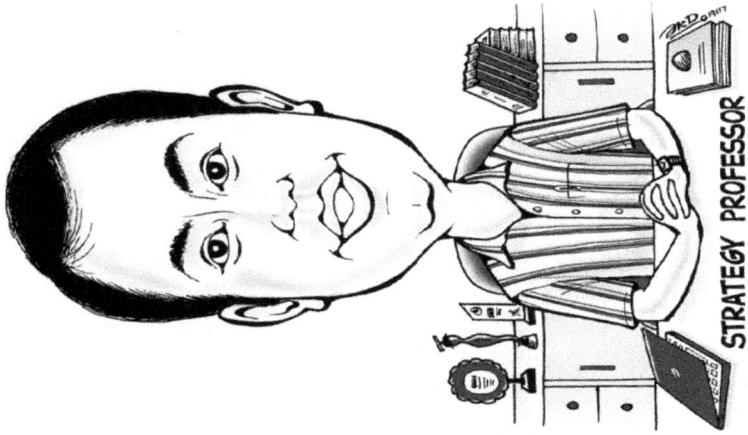

STRATEGY PROFESSOR

Let me share the story of Anna Hazare.

Anna Hazare, after retirement from the Indian army, started improving the ecology and economy of the village "Ralegan Siddhi" using his own money. He organized some like-minded youth of this village as "Tarun Mandal" (youth association) for solving the problems of the village. Ralegan Siddhi is located in the drought-prone Ahmednagar district of Maharashtra state and there were problems of illiteracy, water shortage, alcoholism, and hopelessness. He was able to tackle these problems and turn the village into a model village. Today, he is among the most respected social entrepreneurs.

In India we still have a lot of problems and social entrepreneurship is one answer to solve these.

Take Aways: One need not look at social entrepreneurship as merely charity; one can also make some money while solving social problems.

Your Turn Now: Do you have an idea for social entrepreneurship? Is it sustainable? How can you improve on it?

CHAPTER 30

Entrepreneurial Ecosystem

The Medici Family of Florence and European Renaissance

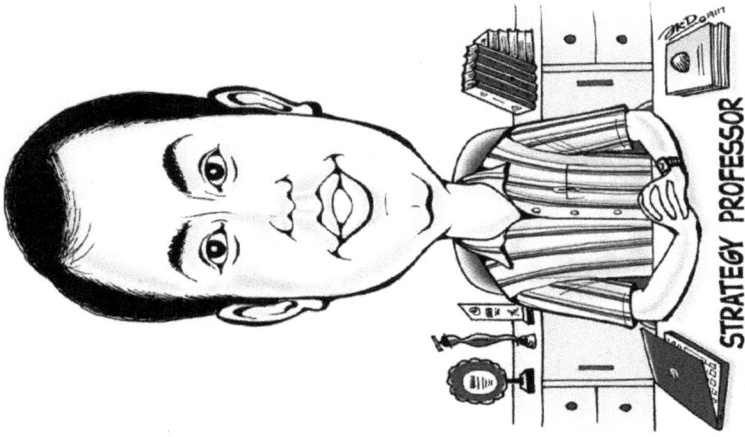

STRATEGY PROFESSOR

The ecosystem matters for startups. Let me present two interesting examples.

The Medici family was a big banking family of Florence in Europe. They financed a lot of artists with different ideas and backgrounds to come and create works of art in Florence. Some historians say this family is a big reason behind the renaissance in Europe. Similarly, the ecosystem of Silicon Valley promotes and supports startups.

Take Aways: If you have a location choice, go for places that have a better ecosystem for startups, particularly in your industry.

Your Turn Now: How is the ecosystem for your startup? Is there any better place with a better ecosystem? How are you taking care of the gaps, if any, in the ecosystem?

Epilogue

Nitish has attended 30 sessions with the founders and the Professor of Strategy. His holidays are over and he is going back to college.

Strategy professor: I hope you have got some ideas about startups.

Nitish: Yes, it was great! I feel I can also create and run a startup successfully.

Strategy professor: Good, you should start working on it.

Nitish: You bet! The three founders have promised me their support in my startup journey. I am just waiting for my exams to be over so that I can start working full-time on my startup. I have already opted out of the campus placement!

A few years later, Nitish is running a successful startup! So are the three founders.

ANNEXURE I

Startup Workbook

Sr. No	Topic
1	Why Startups What is your reason for starting a startup? Is it at least a bit realistic reason? How can you improve on it further?
2	What Startup? What startup do you want to start? Is it at least a bit realistic for success? How can you improve on it further?
3	Entrepreneurial Spirit Do you think you have an entrepreneurial spirit? Why do you think so? How can you improve on it further?
4	Passion—The Nectar of Startups Are you passionate about your startup? Will the passion stay, when you hit the hardships of startups? If yes, why do you think so?
5	Startup Team What should be a good team for your startup? Have you chosen your team as required for success of your startup? Do your team members bring complementary strengths?
6	Resilience Is your team resilient? Why do you think so? How can you improve on it further?
7	Ideation with Innovation Are you innovative? What are you doing for being innovative? How can you improve on it further?
8	Opportunity Sensing and Leveraging How are you going for opportunity sensing and leveraging? Is it correct? How can you improve on it further?
9	Business Model What is your business model? Is it the right one? What it should be?

Sr. No	Topic
10	Niche Focus & Domain Knowledge for Entry Strategy Are you targeting a broad market or a niche segment? What is the entry barrier for others? Is it defensible?
11	Which Product and Market to Go For What is your Ansoff matrix? Is it the right one for you? What it should be?
12	Vanity Metrics Are you using Vanity Metrics? Why are you doing so? What are the correct metrics you should be using?
13	Role of Assumptions What are your assumptions about environment? Are these assumptions correct? How can you improve on it further?
14	Balance between Analysis and Action Do you have a right balance between analysis and action? Why do you think so? What are you doing to achieve this balance?
15	Strategy Do you have a well-defined strategy in place? Does it have elements of regular feedback and improvements? How can you improve on it further?
16	Strategic Thinking: The Fine Art of Balancing Do you have strategic thinking? What are you doing to develop strategic thinking? How can you improve on it further?
17	Organizational Culture Are you able to attract great talent for your startup? What is your strategy for organizational culture? How are you ensuring learning and growth opportunities?
18	Marketing Strategy What is your marketing strategy? Is it good enough? How can you improve on it further?
19	Social Media per se Is Not Marketing Strategy Do you have a social media strategy? Is it in sync with your marketing and overall strategy? How can you improve on it further?
20	Pitch! Is your pitch comprehensive, short, and interesting from the investor perspective? Why do you think so? How can you improve on it further?

21	Financial Strategy Do you have a financial strategy? Are you focusing on delivering results or luxuries? What should be your financial strategy for adding and delivering value?
22	Staying Focused Are you focused? What are you doing to ensure staying away from mindless growth trap? What are you doing to ensure this in future also?
23	Implementation Challenges Are you prepared for possible implementation as well as unseen challenges in the startup journey? Have you put some mechanism or understanding in place to solve these challenges? How can you improve on it further?
24	Pivot Are you madly blindly in love with your startup idea? Is it coming in the way of success of your startup? Are you mentally open for a possible pivot in your startup?
25	Beware of Startup Myths! Are you following startup sayings blindly? Do you have any mechanism to cross-check these sayings? How can you improve on it further?
26	Hedging the Risk Are you using hedging for risk? How are you doing it? What should be the correct hedging you should be using?
27	Entrepreneurial Ecosystem How is the ecosystem for your startup? Is there any better place with a better ecosystem? How are you taking care of the gaps in the ecosystem, if any?

ANNEXURE II

Select Free Resources for More on Startups

Entrepreneurship Simplified: Ashok Soota
https://youtube.com/watch?v=h5palS9vW8g

Guy Kawasaki—The Art of The Start
https://youtube.com/watch?v=7mEQ0ono8mg

The Top 10 Mistakes of Entrepreneurs with Guy Kawasaki
https://youtube.com/watch?v=Oe5c9KK3ZIs

50 Entrepreneurs share priceless advice
https://youtube.com/watch?v=QoqohmccTSc

Guy Kawasaki—The Art of The Start 2.0
https://vimeo.com/125736215

Startup India: The Story of Famous Start-ups Who Dared to Think Different
https://www.youtube.com/watch?v=QSBTaktvYAg

Sachin Bansal on how Flipkart built a Rs 2,000 Cr business in 5 years
https://youtube.com/watch?v=Y70OZ6D4UPg

Startup Rajdhani Bengaluru: Billion-Dollar Club
https://youtube.com/watch?v=7d848kgx20c

Varun Agarwal: From failing in engineering to co-founding a million-dollar company
https://youtube.com/watch?v=nMPqsjuXDmE

References

Story 3. Hindi movie 3 Idiots.

Story 4. Hindi movie Dangal.

Story 5. Hindi movie Lagaan

Story 6. Hindi movie Guru

Story 8. Hindi movie Coolie.

Johansson, F. 2004. *The Medici Effect: Breakthrough Insights at the Intersection of Ideas, Concepts, and Cultures.* Harvard Business Press.

Story 9. http://washingtontimes.com/news/2016/dec/19/bill-clinton-donald-trump-knows-how-to-get-angry-w/(Accessed on March 11, 2017)

Story 10. Pillania, R.K. 2016. *Love Strategy: A New Perspective on Love, Relationships, Life and Strategy.*

Story 11. Hindi movie Special 26.

Story 12. Pillania, R.K. 2016. *Love Strategy: A New Perspective on Love, Relationships, Life and Strategy.*

Story 15. Hindi movie Namaste London.

Story 16. Hindi movie Chak De India

Story 20. Pillania, R. K. 2015. *Strategic Humour: Democratising Strategy.*

Story 21. Hindi movie Rang de Basanti.

Story 22. Two and a Half Men TV Serial.

Story 24. Porter, M.E 1991. "What is Strategy?" *Harvard Business Review.*

Story 27. Pillania, R.K. 2017. "Entrepreneurs Should Know Tricks of the Trade Else They'll Be Running Away with Passbook Vending Machine Instead of ATM." *Business Insider India*, October 17, 2016. http://businessinsider.in/Entrepreneurs-should-know-tricks-of-the-trade-else-theyll-be-running-away-with-passbook-vending-machine-instead-of-ATM/articleshow/54894944.cms

Story 29. www.annahazare.org (accessed March 11, 2017)

Story 30. Johansson, F. 2004. *The Medici Effect: Breakthrough Insights at the Intersection of Ideas, Concepts, and Cultures.* Harvard Business Press.

All stories except no. 10, 11 and 27 are already published in Times of India and The Economic Times blogs.

About the Author

Dr. Rajesh K. Pillania is rated and awarded the Top Professor for Strategy in India by ASSOCHAM and Education Post. He is ranked jointly number one in average research productivity among management faculty (including IIMs/IITs/ISB) in India for research output from 1968 to 2014 (by Prof. Ramdhar Singh of IIM Bangalore and others in 2015). His academic and research experience includes IIM (K), Smith School of Business (Maryland, USA), and Harvard University (Boston, USA) among others. He is Professor of Strategy with MDI, Gurgaon.

Rajesh is passionate about strategy and his areas of expertise are strategy, strategy in India, innovation strategy, global strategy, demystifying strategy, and strategic humor. His research is focused on two broad areas. First one is on frontiers of strategic management and second one is on democratizing strategy. He offers strategic humor workshops, writes for Times of India and The Economic Times, and is a stand-up comedian on strategy. For more visit www.pillania.org and he can be reached at rajesh@pillania.org.

www.ingramcontent.com/pod-product-compliance
Lightning Source LLC
Chambersburg PA
CBHW071840200326
41519CB00016B/4183